Seven Days to Purpose
(Formerly *7 Days in the Life of a Woman*)

Jacqueline Owensby

©Copyright 2012, 2015
Jacqueline Owensby
Women In Need of Empowerment, W.I.N.E.
www.stayonthevine.com
Seven Days to Purpose

All rights reserved. No portion of this booklet may be reproduced, stored or transmitted, in any form or by any means, electronic, mechanical, photocopying, recording or otherwise, without prior written permission of the author.

Published in Hampton, Virginia
Women In Need of Empowerment, Jacqueline Owensby
Cover Illustrations Courtesy of Dream Designs
Graphics: *www.dreamdesignsgraphics.com*

Scripture quotations, unless otherwise noted are taken from the Holy Bible: New Living Translation, 1996, 2004, Tyndale House Publishers, Inc.

Owensby, Jacqueline
Seven Days to Purpose

Inspirational

ISBN-13: 978-0692397190
ISBN-10: 0692397191

Endorsements...

We live in a world that is constantly in motion, everyone appearing to be in a hurry. Have you ever felt like there was something missing in life? How do you start the journey of seeking the MORE in life?

Well ladies . . . prepare for a journey, a mini-retreat where you can read the scriptures and place yourself in a familiar passage to some and a new adventure for others. Jacqueline Owensby allows us to take a glimpse into the life of a woman who was introduced to something so true it instantaneously transformed not only her life but an entire community.

Seven Days to Purpose allows us to see we are in a position of need. We are all thirsty for the truth. Jacqueline has beautifully written these days in parallel with each day God brought creation into being. She compels us to come to the well and be refreshed.

I love the way every woman is be able to relate to Seven Days. I truly believe this book is for every woman based on my experience of serving women all over the world. I am able to apply these simple principals, because as women, we are seeking to fulfill our thirst.

I have personally known Jacqueline for many years and have served with her in several ministry positions. She is authentic and desires to equip women in their lives being transformed through God's word. Read, meditate and ponder the discussion questions with a group of friends. Be prepared to be transformed.

~Martha Stevenson-Jones
International Director Cru (formally Campus Crusade for Christ), Military Ministry, www.militaryministry.org

Jacqueline Owensby is a writer and speaker with one purpose: to serve her King in the ministry of seeing women set free from anything that hinders. She takes notice of others in the race of life and welcomes the opportunity to cheer and encourage. Seven Days to Purpose is evidence of Jacqueline's ability to coach others to excellence in Christ. She masterfully looks into the heart of a woman, exposing the deep motivations hidden there, and inspires the reader to know Christ and her identity in Him.

~Renee Beamer, Author
The Love Triangle: What Every Couple Needs for a Successful Marriage, www.sharingloveandtruth.org

Word for the Reader

I am thrilled you have chosen this interactive study book. My prayer is for us to journey together as we take a look through the eyes of one woman's journey to purpose. She is a woman with no name, simply called the Samaritan Woman, but her circumstances are familiar because she is a woman with a past, who experiences a divine transformation in her present which launches her into her future – into purpose. The past can hinder, causing deep pain and regret. The question is why do we push the tent pegs in deeper and take up residence in the past?

In my humble attempt to share, instruct and provide guidance through one woman's story I cannot help but ask God to give me insight from encounters and yes even my own life that causes women to allow the past to dictate the present, keeping women in an unproductive cycle of regret. Long before I heard this quote I adapted it as one of my personal mantras: "Never let anyone take you back to your past without your permission,"

(S. Brown, 2009). The truth is my past is my testimony, NOT your mallet to beat me over the head with. God loves this Samaritan Woman so much He sent His Son down a dusty path, on a hot, steamy day. In all of her effort to avoid humiliation, shame and loneliness there He sat patiently waiting to heal her emotionally weary heart. This is not only a story of redemption and restoration, but it is an example of what occurs when we finally yield our souls to the Savior.

Seven Days to Purpose takes a unique approach by paralleling the days of creation to the life of the Samaritan Woman. We've heard this familiar message numerous times; it is my objective to examine the process of this woman's journey. Numbers have great significance. I have stumbled across something fascinating in discovering each day of creation can be likened to this woman's journey. From day one of creation to the perfect encounter, the process endured equipped the Samaritan Woman for the purpose she was created to carry. It's time to leave the cycle that has you stuck; drop the bucket, engage purpose.

How to Read this Book

Read with pen and paper nearby, using the study questions and space provided to record your insights, and discuss with a small group. Embrace the healing.

Prep Time: John Chapter 4:1-30; and verses 39-42.

1. Pray: Ask God for understanding

2. Read: With pen in hand

3. Use 5 W's + H: who, what, when, where, why, how

Scripture Reference
John 4:1-30; verses 39-42, NKJV

John 4:1-30
Therefore, when the Lord knew that the Pharisees had heard that Jesus made and baptized more disciples than John (though Jesus Himself did not baptize, but His disciples), He left Judea and departed again to Galilee. But He needed to go through Samaria.

So He came to a city of Samaria which is called Sychar, near the plot of ground that Jacob gave to his son Joseph. Now Jacob's well was there. Jesus therefore, being wearied from His journey, sat thus by the well. It was about the sixth hour.

A woman of Samaria came to draw water. Jesus said to her, "Give Me a drink." For His disciples had gone away into the city to buy food.

Then the woman of Samaria said to Him, "How is it that you, being a Jew, ask a drink from me, a Samaritan woman?" For Jews have no dealings with Samaritans.

Jesus answered and said to her, "If you knew the gift of God, and who it is who says to you, 'Give Me a drink,' you would have asked Him, and He would have given you living water."

The woman said to Him, "Sir, You have nothing to draw with, and the well is deep. Where then do you get that living water? Are you greater than our father Jacob, who gave us the well, and drank from it himself, as well as his sons and his livestock?"

Jesus answered and said to her, "Whoever drinks of this water will thirst again, but whoever drinks of the water that I shall give him will never thirst. But the water that I shall give him will become in him a fountain of water springing up into everlasting life."

The woman said to Him, "Sir, give me this water, that I may not thirst, nor come here to draw."

Jesus said to her, "Go, call your husband, and come here."

The woman answered and said, "I have no husband."

Jesus said to her, "You have well said, 'I have no husband,' for you have had five husbands, and the one whom you now have is not your husband; in that you spoke truly."

The woman said to Him, "Sir, I perceive that you are a prophet. Our fathers worshiped on this mountain, and you Jews say that in Jerusalem is the place where one ought to worship." Jesus said to her, "Woman, believe me, the hour is coming when you will neither on this mountain, nor in Jerusalem, worship the Father. You worship what you do not know; we know what we worship, for salvation is of the Jews. But the hour is coming, and now is, when the true worshipers will worship the Father in spirit and truth; for the Father is seeking such to worship Him. God is Spirit, and those who worship Him must worship in spirit and truth."

The woman said to Him, "I know that Messiah is coming" (who is called Christ). "When He comes, He will tell us all things."

Jesus said to her, "I who speak to you am He."

And at this point His disciples came, and they marveled that He talked with a woman; yet no one said, "What do you seek?" or, "Why are you talking with her?"

The woman then left her water pot, went her way into the city, and said to the men, "Come, see a Man who told me all things that I ever did. Could this be the Christ?" Then they went out of the city and came to Him.

John 4:39-42

And many of the Samaritans of that city believed in Him because of the word of the woman who testified, "He told me all that I ever did." So when the Samaritans had come to Him, they urged Him to stay with them; and He stayed there two days. And many more believed because of His own word.

Then they said to the woman, "Now we believe, not because of what you said, for we ourselves have heard Him and we know that this is indeed the Christ, the Savior of the world."

Introduction

I know this for sure; I can only appreciate where I am because of the journey it took to get me here. Going through those numerous cycles of life reminds me that whatever moment I am experiencing is just that, a moment. We are in constant motion, forever evolving and this season will also pass.

We cannot be as effective when we are constantly looking back. We only look back because the familiar is comfortable. It's time to *engage transformation*. Let's take this walk to the well, alongside our Samaritan sister and get unstuck; let's peel back the layers and loop out of any cycles that are binding and unproductive.

CONTENTS

Day One – What are you Creating	15
Day Two – Unifying Differences	21
Day Three – True Completeness	29
Day Four – Established Order	35
Day Five – Ah Grace	43
Day Six – Encountering the MAN	51
Day Seven – Perfecting Purpose	55
*Now What – New Beginning	61
*A Letter to You	67
*Coach Yourself Through	68
*Meet Him for Yourself	69
*Study Guide/Journal	71
*Quick Points	101

Seven Days to Purpose

Seven Days to Purpose

DAY - ONE

What are you creating?

In the beginning God <u>created</u> the heavens and the earth. Then God <u>said</u>, "Let there be light," and there was light. And God saw that the light was good. Then he <u>separated</u> the light from the darkness. God <u>called</u> the light day and the darkness night.
-Genesis 1:1, 3-5, NLT

How many firsts have you had in your life? First child, first job, first love, the list can go on and on. From the heart of one mother to another, these little darlings do not come with an instruction manual. With that first born I can promise you we goofed on many accounts. We read all of the books, listened to all of the tall tales and still it is a huge learning process full of bumps and bruises in the attempt to fashion this small being into who we think they should be. Sure, you can relate to taking a situation you feel has reached crisis mode into your own hands for the sake of making things fit better into your world.

There's an extensive amount of time spent creating and conjuring up something again and again only to be disappointed with the outcome. This creation process can be daunting. When we peer into the life of our Samaritan sister we can only imagine how stunned she was when the Lord Himself in the middle of a conversation asks her to, *Go, call your husband and then come back.* When you know not only is the one you're with not your own but neither were the ones before, it makes the matter a bit awkward. But let's not hang our hat too soon.

The first response I have to this is one of total shock. This woman goes to the well in the heat of the day. When I was growing up, my Grandma used a well or a pump to get water from daily for cooking or washing. I begin to ponder this and realized she always went early morning or late evening, but rarely in the heat of the day.

The Samaritan Woman went to the well during the hottest part of the day when most likely no townspeople would be there. When we do not want to be seen, heard or spoken to we will take a round-a-bout way to accomplish the easiest of tasks. Let's be real, if I am having an off day I will drive to an entirely different neighborhood or part of the city to go to the grocery store if it means I can avoid those familiar faces that remind me of my worth. It's piping hot outside and she is at the well drawing water. Then, during what she initially thought to be a casual conversation with a stranger, her life story is laid out before her. Can you imagine this happening to you?

Think about it, this woman has a past she is not particularly proud of; she has endured a cycle of events that has led to her need to avoid others. Her number one ended as a result of her own strength failing to create a favorable outcome. The question is what is your #1? What is it that you have failed at in your attempt to create something in your own strength?

Loneliness can trigger a myriad of feelings. One mistake is to label loneliness as depression because of the emotional state of mind this feeling promotes. Loneliness can lead to bitterness and a state of desperation which can be the motivating factor that drives an individual to conjuring up and settling for a cheap imitation. We put ourselves through this vain process only to discover that our ways and our thoughts are not aligned to Gods. The Creator has to be first before we can move forward in creating anything. It is He who divinely inspires giving us Heavenly downloads for every broken area of our lives.

The word creation means to *fashion anew*. God renewed what was in a state of chaos. The number one denotes beginning, first, or the start of something. *In the beginning God <u>created</u>* . . . this is a statement to cling fast to because it offers hope and security which cannot be challenged by any situation that might arise in life.

DAY ONE: DIGGING DEEPER:

Scriptures tell us day one is the day of creation. If you look at this passage again you learn nothing was present. All was empty and void. The only thing was God, the Spirit and the Word that would transform Gods thoughts into reality. When most women are empty and needing fulfillment, they attempt to create something. Now, most desire to create something good. But the truth be told, a bad thing is better than nothing in a person's mind if they become lonely enough. So we begin to settle and lower standards; overlooking the fact, that key components are missing in who or what we are attempting to connect with - all in an effort to avoid loneliness.

When God began creating something out of nothing, He not only had exactly what He wanted to create in mind, but He also had the power and wisdom to control and handle the very thing He created. One of the things we lack is the ability to control and handle another person. You see, we are not the creator of mankind. Therefore, we don't have the power to control another. The best we can do is better ourselves and live by an unwavering standard. We must forever keep in the forefront of our minds to be careful in our pursuits as we go about the concept of creating in our own lives. We are always creating something. The question is "what" are we creating? Will this bring us the satisfaction we so yearn to have? Will we look back upon what we have created and be able to say – it's good.

DAY - TWO

Unifying Differences

Then God said, "Let there be a space between the waters, to separate the waters of the heavens from the waters of the earth." And that is what happened. God called the space "sky." And evening passed and morning came, marking the second day.
-Genesis 1:6-8, NLT

There is space between the waters to separate waters from the heavens, calling the space sky. Though there is obvious division occurring here, it is within the frame of "unifying" differences; bringing order to disorder.

The number two indicates unity and division here. Each step of separation brings order out of the chaos and is a testimony of God's great wisdom and power. His perception is far deeper than ours. Many times we can have super intentions to bring peace and order to a situation only to end up adding more confusion. Why? Our ways are not like His. We see this time and time again when we set out to make a decision out of our pain, which leads to making a permanent decision over something that was intended to pass.

As a single woman loneliness and fear can create the temptation to strike out and make something happen. This results in compromising values all in the name of filling that gaping hole. But I want to take a moment to caution any single woman reading this section on unity. You do not have to settle! Your standards, when aligned with God's are not too high and your values when in His will are in the right place. There is no permanent gratification in settling and lowering your expectations so that you can snuggle up next to a pair of biceps.

At some point we all realize the importance of living in harmony; be it with ourselves or with another. This motivates us to naturally set out on a mission to pursue being unified with someone or something – because we were created to connect. We are attempting to connect the dots in life. While planning is a good thing, we must move with caution always remaining flexible to the will of God first. Clearly, scripture reminds us to *seek Him first;* we do not want to put the cart before the horse. God wants your heart to be hidden deep in Him – this is a place of safety.

Now, I am imagining the Samaritan Woman was attempting to implement a bit of unity in her life after her first attempt to create failed. Let's put ourselves in her shoes for a moment and walk with her. She meets a man at a well where she confesses that not even the fifth man she is with is her husband. She has gone through a cycle she somehow cannot loop out of. Caution! Let's not get hung up on the fact the woman has had five men, (relationships), instead let's examine this from the aspect of the numerous cycles she's been through.

When you read John Chapter 4, we must ask the question, what about the other four. Numbers are important and hold great meaning. We pick up with number five, but let's go back in our own minds eye and examine the former. Perhaps there is some clue as to why she keeps returning to the same place, in the same cycle over and over again. Perhaps there is something there that will help aide even me in my personal desire to loop out of a cycle I may be enduring.

Asking why I am still in this repetitive mess of attracting the same kind of man is a matter worthy of exploring. Ladies it's quite simple, we tend to attract who we are - in most cases. At some point we've all made that familiar vow not to date any more. Maybe due to disappointing and traumatic relationships or perhaps the examples we've grown up with in our own homes and communities. Trauma can cause you to continue to do the same thing over and over while expecting life to change around you. Trauma can cause you to want to do what is safe, which locks you into a vicious cycle. Where did the disciple Peter say he was going not long after Jesus had been crucified? Peter said, *I'm going fishing,* (John 21:3). This was "familiar" and soothing for him to go back, to return to what is familiar even though experiences and life has proven it will never be the same again. What is that has you so tangled up that you keep returning to that place for comfort?

Sometimes experience can be the best teacher. However, because some of us are quick learners and low on tolerance we plunge head first vowing never to date again until it is to the man we will marry. I even said that I would join a convent first. Sounds funny today but when you begin to refocus and redirect who and what you are connecting to it requires a made up mind. All of our striving for unity can become disastrous when we are not being led by the One who is the master at unifying; God did so by unifying through division. Did you get that? Pause and really consider this concept. He who separated the waters from the heavens knew exactly what it would take to bring harmony into existence. God did so with a "word", He said *let there be*; the dilemma is not necessarily what we are allowing to run in and out of our lives, but rather what we are speaking into our lives.

DAY TWO: DIGGING DEEPER

Space: One of the things that allow us the opportunity to know who we are is space. Before God created space, everything ran together. Everything looked as if it was a part of something else. There was no distinction. Key factors could not be identified. When there is no space or distinction, we wrap everything together and we choose how it will be identified. In other words, he is nice, cute, has a great job, treats me nice most times, and only hits me when he is angry, but he is a good man. Do you see the blurred lines? Another thing about space and separation is it allows you to see what makes you special and it helps others to appreciate that. This is why it is so important that we remain true to who we are over imitating others and crossing into their lane. Each of us have been given our own race to run. God made us special and He often separates us from the crowd so that we can use those differences for His glory. Where one is weak, the other is strong.

The Samaritan Woman may have been seeking unity in her number two, but somewhere along this path she discovered the lines were not blurring together, the differences instead were being magnified in her own doing. Only the Master Creator is able to unify differences in perfect harmony.

DAY - THREE

True Completeness

Then God said, "Let the waters under the heavens be gathered together into one place, and let the dry land appear"; and it was so. And God called the dry land Earth, and the gathering together of the waters He called Seas. Then God said, "Let the earth bring forth grass, the herb that yields seed, and the fruit tree that yields fruit according to its kind, whose seed is in itself, on the earth"; and it was so. And God saw that it was good. So the evening and the morning were the third day.

-Genesis 1:9-13, NLT

These verses give us a description of the third day again revealing the power and wisdom of our God to bring order to chaos; through separation He creates unity. He put everything in place for humanity, according to His own design and said it was good – meaning final, done, carried out, and complete. In fact, when Jesus was sitting by that well in Samaria having a casual conversation with a woman who most would have shunned, I like to think He was bringing order to the chaos that existed in her life. Through her isolation and separation of community He was creating unity in one person, making things right and complete again.

Let's take a closer look at completeness: we are complete in that we have a spirit that lives in a body that has a soul; whole and complete. Yet, we seek wholeness in everything around us except God Himself. We look to other "things" to satisfy and mold us into the image we desire. How many times have we wrapped our identity up in someone or thing; job, sports, economic status.

I can recall that wonderful agreement made during those honeymoon years, proclaiming that I would stop working and remain in the home until our children began school. Great idea, easier said than done. So we place these high demands before us and then we begin the bargaining process with God trying to get out of keeping our own word. Revelation: we are not going to change His mind no matter how long we fast and pray, but we will gain a greater appreciation, closeness and indeed a higher level of trust in Him. I took three personal days from work to seek the Lord on whether or not I heard Him say resign. Go ahead and laugh; it's quite hysterical. Those three days were spent crying because I already knew the answer; but fasting did position me to obey because the flesh was weak. Completion in action! Yet. I wasted a lot of time seeking the answers in others. Society has a way of slowing shaping your perception and molding you to fit the world's standards.

When Jesus was on the cross bearing all for us; He uttered some powerful words when he said, *"it is finished,"* (John 19:30). He was saying it is fulfilled, I have done all required; I have run this race to the finish. Many times when this picture is painted in our minds we get images of a weak, weary Savior. I'd like to suggest we take another look and consider who was uttering these words. The Almighty Anointed One said, *it is finished* because everything that was necessary was done -

complete. The thought to ponder is have we done all that is necessary?

DAY THREE: DIGGING DEEPER

One of the best things about being alone is that we can work on us. Sad to say, many of us do not take this opportunity. We spend our "alone" days feeling depressed or doing things so that we can feel complete. Maybe it's shopping, or inhaling a tub of your favorite ice-cream and ribs. The best thing that you can do as a woman is to become complete before you link up with someone else.

Allow God to show you, grow you, and mold you. He wants to show you who you are, the empty and weak spots and what you need to do to become whole. In His hands, the lump of clay that we call life is molded into a beautiful pot that others can appreciate and He can use.

Because we were once separated from God, we were filled with darkness and empty space. When we said "I do" to the Lord, He placed His bright light into our lives. The light reveals the empty, dark spots. Did you get that? The light "reveals" the empty spots. It does not fill them. Therefore, when the light starts showing you the empty spots in your life; that is not a time to have regrets or stand in denial. That is a time to understand and seek filling. God's desire is not for you to be empty but for you to be filled - filled with His joy, His peace and His provision.

Our Samaritan sister was perhaps looking to have true completeness and like some of us maybe learned that this type of completeness, this type of focused harmony fashioning chaos into completeness requires keen focus. Sometimes we grow weary in this process and find it easiest to move on to whose next. There's a momentary lightness for some when they quit that relationship or job. Then the truth settles in and life crashes in reminding you that the process was actually incomplete after all.

Seven Days to Purpose

DAY - FOUR

Established Order

Then God said, "Let lights appear in the sky to separate the day from the night. Let them mark off the seasons, days, and years. Let these lights in the sky shine down on the earth. God made two great lights—the larger one to govern the day, and the smaller one to govern the night. He also made the stars. God set these lights in the sky to light the earth, to govern the day and night, and to separate the light from the darkness. And God saw that it was good. And evening passed and morning came, marking the fourth day.

-Genesis 1:14-19, NLT

By day four we see an even greater display of God's power. He alone placed the sun, moon and stars into a perfect tempo. This was not done so that we debate over how, when and where, but instead to usher us into relationship with our Creator. Everything He has set in place has purpose and the primary purpose of all things is to bring Him Glory, to worship Him alone.

Now in utter amazement I am still wondering that if the stars, moon and sun get this concept of worship, the gratification of purpose, then why are we still "stuck"? This fabulous essence of light shines in total devotion of the Creator; beaming brightly in honor of God's power. Even the mountains rise and the trees sway in awe, the birds chirp and wind blows with great purpose. Yet we are stuck, stuck, stuck. Stuck in our past issues and present failures. It is because of this we are not bringing God Glory, we are not honoring our Creator and we are not bearing good fruit through our divine purpose.

No wonder this woman was going to the well in the heat of the day. Not only was she avoiding crossing the path of those who shunned and talked about her, but she was not able to bring God Glory in her current state – she was not connected to purpose. So, like the Samaritan woman when we finally come clean, when we own up to the truth and we answer God with raw boldness, do we realize this place of stuck is not what I was created for and we want out. She returned to the same place, doing the same thing for so long yearning for change. Do you really believe she wanted to be in the situation she was in?

The number four represents the natural order of things, evokes solidity, calmness and refers to all that is created. For example we have four elements (earth, air, fire and water), four regions (north, south, east and west), four divisions of our day (morning, noon, evening and midnight), there are four seasons (spring, summer, autumn and winter). I am certain the list goes on and on and we could spend a lot of time discussing the parallels of the number four as it relates to scripture. The point being made is we serve an omnipotent God whose knowledge and wisdom is so immense that we cannot begin to comprehend the knowledge of our God, though we experience His power daily as we live, move and breathe.

Let's imagine how our Samaritan sister feels by the

time she encounters number four. By now she is getting quite tired of being sick and tired. All she wants is some type of solidity in life. Can you relate to this where you are in this cycle of life? Life has a way of throwing things at us so fast we barely have time to recover from the first knock down or disappointment before we are getting slapped again. There's no time to recover from the last hit. We begin to think if anything is going to change it's going to be because I make it change versus us simply surrendering to the process of change. We get to that place where we simply want to say enough already. We are treading water and this can be a dangerous.

In the case with our sister the Samaritan woman she was obviously tired and withdrawn to the point she opted to simply use avoidance as her method to survival. What methods do we use? How do we cope when we have lost the order of things in life and there is no peace, no control at all? When we further examine this number it brings to light the model of relationship. You see when God created this natural order of things be it stars, moon, sun, seasons or elements; I believe each object performs with total perfection and in absolute harmony according to their own purpose. The purpose is to shine and their service is to Him first. We too are created to do what God created us to do. We must ask ourselves, is our service to God shining brightly for Him or mankind?

DAY FOUR: DIGGING DEEPER

The natural order of things: In simple terms, that means the way things are supposed to happen. Sometimes we cannot or do not allow things to happen naturally because of the resistance we feel regarding past encounters.

This reminds me of the concept surrounding cause and effect. I burn my finger on the gas stove and because of this I now have an issue with gas stoves. When I move into a new house my first quest is to find out if that house has a gas stove. In my mind I am saying the electric stove is safer. Not necessarily, I just got careless and fire burns.

One of the enemy's greatest weapons is "abortion". If he can kill a dream, a thought, a gift, or talent before it gets life then he does not have to worry about the dream maturing. Keep in mind Satan doesn't mind you staying busy doing good things. But what he does mind is you walking in your purpose, because that's when your life makes hell shake. What has happened to you that caused you to say "I will never do that, or I will never attempt anything like that again? This is one of the reasons God brought light. Many times in our lives we encounter only darkness and we attempt to build our lives accordingly. But why would we want to mold our life based on a bad experience. Light comes to reveal not only the unfavorable areas but it also shows there is another way. His way! Know that the enemy is a thief and he sees what God has in store for you and so he comes to *kill, steal and destroy,* (John 10:10), the plan before it takes flight. He knows if he can get the carrier of the gift to give up hope prior to lift off, he wins.

My husband had a terrible experience in elementary school. He was one of the top spellers in his fourth grade class and was chosen to represent the class in the school spelling bee. When he stood on stage and looked at all of the people from his school sitting there waiting for him to spell a two syllable word, he froze. Long story short, he misspelled the word and was eliminated from the competition. His immature, fourth grade mind told him he was not able to perform or talk in front of crowds. So, for years he struggled with speaking in public. Then came the light. He sought God for help in this area and was reminded of that day. The enemy's plan was to abort his purpose and gift. But Gods plan and purpose must go forth; all we must do is properly position ourselves even if it's at a well in the heat of the day and ask for His help, for His everlasting water so we no longer thirst.

DAY - FIVE

AH GRACE

Then God said, "Let the waters swarm with fish and other life. Let the skies be filled with birds of every kind." So God created great sea creatures and every living thing that scurries and swarms in the water, and every sort of bird—each producing offspring of the same kind. And God saw that it was good. Then God blessed them, saying, "Be fruitful and multiply. Let the fish fill the seas, and let the birds multiply on the earth." And evening passed and morning came, marking the fifth day.

-Genesis 1:20-23, NLT

We enter into day five and there is one word that rings strong in this text; fruitfulness. Bearing fruit is the blessing of the Lord! Not any fruit but fruit after its <u>own</u> kind, even in the number five there is unity, harmony and order. The number five paints a picture of "grace". Let's back up a minute so that we can have total

understanding. The number four represents the natural order. This order can only come from the hand of God. When you consider all we have shared regarding the order of the earth and the chaos in one woman's life we see this clearly.

In our natural state we are weak and hopeless but when God sets our lives in order we begin to operate in a manner that not only lifts our very being but brings Him glory and honor because we are then operating from that place of purpose. The number five is for grace which is also called "favor". The favor of God rests upon you! No matter what your hurdle you must leap over it. His grace is sufficient because we are divinely favored.

But what does this really mean? "His grace is sufficient for me," (II Corinthians 12:9). Grace has many forms of favor which is extended to us. For you grace may be covering unworthy state of need where God's favor is demonstrated in the mercy He grants you to breathe again when you have deliberately disobeyed Him. His grace can take on many forms to accommodate the need. Grace is what enables you to continue running the race no matter what obstacles you face. Grace is like a defibrillator, which is used to control the heart by applying an electric current to the chest or to the heart so that you continue to get the movement required for life.

So it is with our Samaritan sister. God's grace was the electric current she needed to jump start her purpose. When we finally discover nothing we have or nothing we have done has resulted in the peace of God and His boundless fruit flowing through us, unworthiness causes us to want to give up. So we pick up one thing and put it down, then we pick up another thing and put it down and the cycle continues whether it's a man or business venture. And we keep starting over and over and over just as she had done. We dare not look down upon this woman; Christ quickly acknowledges her current state of being when He confirms she had answered Him truthfully because she has had five husbands and the one (number 6), she is with is not her own. Wow! This woman was seeking a bit of grace at this point; yes peace would be nice but how about a bit of grace extended from the One whose favor is limitless. I have heard it preached that "favor ain't fair" and this simply means we can press through any barrier with favor and walk through any valley when the favor of the Lord is upon us. His favor opens doors no man can shut, His favor extends opportunities no man can comprehend, His favor promotes without degrees or experience and His favor connects us to healthy, loving and lasting relationships. His favor reveals purpose.

There is one final example I'd like to leave you with regarding God's grace and favor toward us. The Bible gives us wonderful examples and numbers are used extensively throughout these teachings on grace. Let's think back for a moment on the state of mind the Samaritan Woman might have been in at this time.

Shunned by others, inadequate and feeling ashamed to the point where she doesn't even want to encounter

people. This is enough to make a person want to be at war with themselves and anyone attempting to cross their path.

There is another who must have felt this same type of offense from others; one we call David. He must have gotten pretty worked up due to the shame his people was being put through after the taunting of that Philistine Giant. David understood something not yet embraced fully by the Samaritan Woman. David understood not only who he was but he understood whose He was. The Bible tells us David gathered 5 smooth stones (I Samuel 17:40-51), but he only needed to use one to take out that giant of shame that was linked to a constant reminder of failure, a reminder of being stuck. Once again God's grace truly is sufficient. He is able to use what appears weak and feeble, lost and hopeless and add His divine power to that which results in His unmerited favor. Point made: "Favor ain't fair," but is sure is just.

The Samaritan woman was being bathed in Gods favor because she was discovering that purpose deep within her that would bring Him Glory. God's grace was literally washing her as they engaged in conversation; healing and restoration was taking place.

DAY FIVE: DIGGING DEEPER

Grace has nothing to do with you. You can't earn it. You can't make it. You can't take it. You can only receive it. It is unmerited (undeserved) favor. Now, this brings a few thoughts to mind.

God created these animals whose sole purpose was to be fruitful and multiply. God created them and set them in place without your help. The only thing you could do is accept them. They did not come because you were worthy or unworthy. They did not come because you were good or bad. They came because they were created by God, who intended them to be fruitful and multiply. There are times when things come into your life that have absolutely nothing to do with you or your works. They are in your life to be fruitful, to create multiplication.

God has a way of working it all for your good, to multiply abundance in your life. Grace has nothing to do with your labor. The problem is, like this Samaritan Woman we feel the need to look for what we "think" we are worth versus allowing Grace to bring us what "He" is worth.

DAY - SIX

Encountering the MAN

Then God said, "Let the earth produce every sort of animal, each producing offspring of the same kind," And God saw that it was good. Then God said, "Let us make human beings in our image," So God created human beings in his own image. In the image of God he created them; male and female he created them. Then God blessed them and said, "Be fruitful and multiply. Fill the earth and govern it. Reign over the fish in the sea, the birds in the sky, and all the animals that scurry along the ground.
-Genesis 1:24-28, NLT

We are made in the image of God and He placed mankind on the earth to oversee all creation. We are placed here to reign over all God has made, to be fruitful and to multiply. We learn God labored six days and on this day man was created. The number six denotes labor and imperfection. I almost want to repeat that because we will skim right over that revelation. The number six denotes "labor" and "imperfection". Let's park here for a moment.

Man, humankind was created on day six and given six days to labor. So there's the creation of man on day six followed by God's rest. Humankind fell short of the perfection. God alone is perfect, all powerful, in control and self-sufficient.

Labor is simply physical or mental exertion, (free dictionary.com). When I consider the term labor based upon the idea that God created mankind one thought comes to mind as a woman. Eve! She labored in pain – she exerted physical and mental energy in the life-bearing process. As women we can relate to "labor" whether we have physically birthed forth a child or simply cared for one. There is a process from carrying the child, to experiencing the labor pains, to final birthing of the child. We can relate to this process of exertion. The question is what lies deep within you waiting to be birthed, waiting to be manifested here in this earth for all to bear witness of and partake of? God created mankind with purpose in mind. Ephesians 2:10 confirms, *"For we are God's masterpiece. He created us anew in Christ, so we can do the good things He planned for us long ago."*

Our Samaritan sister falls right into position when she strolls in the heat of the day to the well for water. All of that hiding out and avoiding people was a set up on this particular day for the purpose within her to be awakened. She walked right into the arms of the One who had the key to unlocking the chains of bondage that kept her looping through life unfruitful and hopeless. In her imperfection, she collided with His perfection and the light overtook the darkness!

Imperfection is having a fault, blemish-tarnished, stained. Women are life-bearers and in order to have a life of purpose it is of great importance to abide in Him. To sit, to dwell, to live in and to stay connected to God. It is only when we are connected to Him that we are able to truly be fruitful and multiply.

DAY SIX: DIGGING DEEPER

What kind of people do you draw into your life? One of the key things about life is the law that says you will produce after your own kind. What are you producing? What or who are you attracting? Earlier we stated, most people attract who they are. If you are attracting the wrong type of people into your life, check "your" crop, make the necessary adjustments, and watch your circle of influence. It's time to change for the better.

DAY - SEVEN

Perfecting Purpose

So the creation of the heavens and the earth and everything in them was completed. On the seventh day God had finished his work of creation, so he rested from all his work.

-Genesis 2:1-2, NLT

Research tells us the number seven is one of the most frequent numerals in the Bible. We learn here that on the seventh day all was done and God rested; the number seven represents spiritual perfection and completeness. After all His "labor" God rested acknowledging His work was picture perfect and whole. But let the record reflect again, God did not need to rest because He grew weary. He rested because, "it was all good". Everything was given His is stamp of approval.

Let's revisit the Samaritan Woman. Jesus asked her to go get her husband and she replied she did not have a husband. Jesus agreeing with her stated she has had five and the one she is currently with is not her own. Now you do the math! She is at number six and this woman is due her rest. On this day, day seven, at that well, she runs into the perfect One. The One who will give her rest; the One who will quench that aching thirst!

We are not certain as to what caused this woman to endure such disappointment in life, to be shunned and humiliated, ashamed and more than likely talked about to the point she would rather strike out on a road march to get water in the blazing sun. I submit to you that we, yes, you and I have some "thing" that we too would rather hide under a rock. But Jesus would not have this woman live bound and stuck any longer. He would not have any of us live with an invisible hand over our face suffocating the life out of us because of shame, loneliness, or heartache. Beloved, He loves you too much.

The truth is many of us would not recognize perfection if it walked up to us and slapped us in the face because of all the pain we still carry today. I do not mind sharing this with you because it is part of my own example of God's abounding grace and love. My growing up was challenging at times – oh the good far outweighs the bad; but Papa was a rolling stone and Mama reaped a bit of abuse from time to time. It took my Mother 13 times of leaving and returning before she finally said, ENOUGH; not going back. She too had an encounter and decided to loop out of a cycle.

As a young girl growing up in the country I was trying to find myself much like the next young girl. Because the love in my household far outweighed the indifferences I was able to develop into an emotionally stable and happy young lady by the time I left home. Any infractions, mishaps or wayward acts on my part was usually not due to the lack of teaching or the lack of love from my parents. In short, it was due to my own personal ignorance and selfishness. God's love has always been prevalent in my life and my parents displayed God's love toward me daily. I believe this is what has kept me over the years. I believe this is what kept my Samaritan sister. It was the love that someone showed at some point in her life that gave her strength to put one foot in front of the other each day, even if it meant going to draw water from the well alone.

One day when we reach that final breaking point, that place where you say enough already and you have an attitude that says I don't care what anyone thinks I just want to be free. Then God will meet you in the heat of your situation and give you what you are thirsting for – life.

John 4:4 reads, Jesus needed to go through Samaria. He NEEDED to go. For that one, He detoured, He stopped in the sweltering heat and said let's get you unstuck little sister. He sent the disciples on into town and covered this woman with His love. Let's get you out of this cycle - the Father has need of you.

DAY SEVEN: DIGGING DEEPER

That's perfect. The word "perfect" is often misunderstood and sneered at by people because of the connotations behind it. Expressing that something is "perfect" does not mean it is flawless, without blemish, or that it cannot be improved in some way. Perfect has a lot more to do with maturity than it does with the outcome. Do you know when to stop? Do you know when to say enough is enough? Think about your current relationships. Do you have any that you should have ended long ago? Think about your eating habits, your health. Do you know when it is time to exercise, when it is time to push away from the table? Think about your job, do you know when it is time to "change" positions. The Samaritan woman, though initially doubtful, had an ear to hear and decided the time had come to make a change, to release her imperfections for Christ's perfection. Perfect.

Seven Days to Purpose

Now What?

New Beginning

... anyone who belongs to Christ has become a new person. The old life is gone; a new life has begun, (II Corinthians 5:17)

It is unwise and immature for us to measure our growth by the experiences and growth of another. You being in Christ are new and the old is gone. Can you imagine how this woman felt carrying the burden of yesterday every waking moment of her life? Each day she rose her past rose with her, she didn't have to strap it on because it was attached and fixated to her. So much so that all she could do was see the outer person who stood in front of her at the well – a Jew. She was so caught up in her own moment of crisis if Jesus had not followed through she would have returned home with the water she had come to draw and missed out on the well of life that was sitting in her presence.

Aren't you glad that He doesn't give up on us? Christ pursues us relentlessly and He does so with such style, care and candor. Each of us when we say "I Do" to the hand of Christ, have decided to release the old and embrace the new. The past belongs in the past because all it does is cripple the present and abort the future. One reason you are here is to glorify God through your divinely given purpose!

In order to do so you must understand these two truths: 1. Come clean - as the Samaritan woman did at the well; and 2. Trust God's chosen purpose.

The Samaritan Woman offers us an example of how tender our loving God is toward us. She experiences numerous cycles in life. I am thinking that all she wanted was to know who she really was and in some way perhaps she was spinning in this cycle by seeking this confirmation through the many relationships she had experienced. Isn't this just like us dear sisters. Seeking answers from man for confirmation. How many times have you said at the start of a new year that you were going to do things different this time?

We are not given her name or history or even how old she is. All we know is that she is a woman with a past. That point is made very clear. She is a woman who more than likely had some unfavorable experiences in life. Nevertheless, from the scriptures we see she is bold and intelligent enough to hold her own in a conversation even with a Jew. She even makes it very clear that obviously Jews and Samaritans have nothing to do with each other. Not only that, but notice she is alone at the well with "a man". Oh my, what would the townspeople say about her this time.

This dear woman didn't stand a chance in the presence of the Christ. Her snippy attitude and strong voice led her right in to her niche. Jesus was coaching her right into purpose and here she was probably thinking she was in control of the entire conversation.

It would be naïve of anyone to look upon this woman with eyes of pity or scorn. I say so because if we examine the conversation closely that she had with the Savior we will see this Samaritan Woman in an entirely new light. She was not a passive woman. Think about that for a moment. She had dealings with the community of people she was in – yes this woman knew how to talk to a man; remember she had several personal interactions already. Another point to note about the Samaritan Woman is that she knew how to exercise her voice and was smart about it. The woman engaged in a debate with the Son of God. Finally, she was the one who received Christ's living water and went to shout about it, yes I would guess even to the one that was not her husband.

She then does something else that simply makes me scream with joy. The woman who came bearing a heavy load, who came carrying that bucket full of issues steps out of a cycle of hopelessness into hope. She stepped out of fear and became fearless. Ah yes, this sister-girl was a very smart woman, smart enough to recognize opportunity was knocking and she released that bucket of shame and opened her hands to purpose.

This entire interpretation moves me deep down in the depths of my core. The story of the Samaritan Woman is a story about rebirth. This is one woman's story about how she came back and rose from the ashes. You must understand that her story is every woman's story. It is the story of starting over again in a season where you have been revived to bloom and flourish.

Digging Deeper:

The number 7 = perfection and the number 1 = the beginning. Together these are explosive in ushering in the new order of things. Our Samaritan sister had no clue that while she was in conversation with an initial stranger, His words were washing her, giving her a deep cleaning and a new beginning. She went to the well to get water, had a conversation with perfection, came clean, and was launched into her new beginning, leaving her water pot and walking into doing good works. She returns to the city transformed and tells all about a man who told her all things she'd ever done. *Could this be the Christ*, (John 4:29)? Did you get that first part? She returned to the very was she was avoiding.

A Letter to You . . .

My dear sister if you have taken the time to read or maybe you simply skimmed through this little token of inspiration it is my hope that you found yourself on one of those days, in one of those cycles. The good news is you do not have to stay in that place of trying to create the unity, peace, harmony, joy, attention or satisfaction you are attempting to gain on your own. No more seeking confirmation from someone or something that simply cannot deliver this type of fullness. Only God can fill the void in your life, those holes you've so desperately tried to repair.

A fulfilled woman is a woman who is living in divine purpose. There are others waiting on you – you are waiting on you. So why not start today by coaching yourself through the process of ending the cycle and beginning again.

Coach Yourself Through . . .

1. Identify the cycle?

2. What junk are you still carrying?

3. How does this make you feel?

4. How would you like to move forward?

5. Describe what starting over looks like?

6. What's one thing you can do now to begin again?

7. What's holding you back from a fresh start?

8. How can you maneuver this obstacle?

9. What will you do to begin again?

10. Go do it!

Meet Him for Yourself . . .

If you are reading this book and you have not made a commitment to follow after His heart, please know you do not have to go to a well, in the heat of the day to meet perfection. He will meet you right now, right where you are. If you are willing to open your heart to Him say this prayer aloud:

Dear God, I acknowledge that I am a sinner and I am sorry for my sins and the life I've lived disconnected from you; I need your forgiveness. I believe Your Son Jesus died, was buried and rose again for me to have life everlasting. I confess Jesus as the Lord of my soul and with my heart I accept Jesus Christ as my own personal Savior. Thank you Jesus, for your grace that has saved me from a life of darkness and turned me to your marvelous light. Romans 10:9-10 says, "If you confess with your mouth the Lord Jesus and believe in your heart that God has raised Him from the dead, you will be saved. For with the heart one believes unto righteousness, and with the mouth confession is made unto salvation." Because I have done this I am now a new creature, the old man is buried and all things have been made new.

So you said the prayer! You are ready to launch into the next phase of building this relationship with Christ. Get connected to a Bible-based teaching ministry and study God's word. Surround yourself with others of like faith so that you can draw strength from the power of connecting. Go tell someone right now you are a new creature! Finally, we would love to hear from you. Contact us at: ***info@stayonthevine.com*** or visit us on the web: ***www.stayonthevine.com*** and join our mailing list for inspirational resources and upcoming events.

STUDY GUIDE/JOURNAL

Seven Days to Purpose

Study Guide:

Chapter One: Creation

1. What are you attempting to do in your own strength?

   _____

   _____

   _____

2. What results is this bringing you? Lasting or temporal?

   _____

   _____

   _____

3. Explain in your own words the following scripture: Matthew 6:33

   _____

   _____

   _____

JOURNAL ABOUT IT ...

What are you going to do to apply the concept of creating the life you want?

_____
_____
_____
_____
_____
_____
_____
_____
_____
_____
_____
_____
_____
_____
_____
_____

Seven Days to Purpose

Chapter Two: Unity

1. In what ways are you compromising your standards within current relationships?

   _____

   _____

   _____

2. What is your first response to trauma - to go back to what's familiar or press on?

   _____

   _____

   _____

3. What did Peter do in John 21:3-6 and why do you think he did so?

   _____

   _____

   _____

   _____

   _____

   _____

Seven Days to Purpose

JOURNAL ABOUT IT . . .

What are you going to do to apply the concept of exercising unity in your life?

Seven Days to Purpose

Chapter Three: Completeness

1. What areas of your life do you consider incomplete?

   _____

   _____

   _____

2. What areas of your life do you consider complete?

   _____

   _____

   _____

3. Explain in your own words what it means to you when Christ said "It is finished," John 19:30.

   _____

   _____

   _____

   _____

   _____

   _____

Seven Days to Purpose

JOURNAL ABOUT IT . . .

What are you going to do to apply the concept of living a life of wholeness/completeness in your life?

_____
_____
_____
_____
_____
_____
_____
_____
_____
_____
_____
_____
_____
_____
_____
_____

Seven Days to Purpose

Chapter Four: Order

1. Have you accepted Jesus as your personal savior? If yes, when?

    _____

    _____

    _____

2. What was your biggest challenge in turning from the old ways to embrace the new?

    _____

    _____

    _____

3. Explain God's knowledge of us according to: Psalm 139:1-14

    _____

    _____

    _____

    _____

    _____

    _____

Seven Days to Purpose

Seven Days to Purpose

JOURNAL ABOUT IT . . .

What are you going to do to gain order in your life?

_____
_____
_____
_____
_____
_____
_____
_____
_____
_____
_____
_____
_____
_____
_____
_____
_____

Seven Days to Purpose

Chapter Five: Grace

1. What is that thing that keeps gnawing at you — that thorn in your side?

   _____

   _____

   _____

2. What would be the ideal solution for your deliverance from this thorn?

   _____

   _____

   _____

3. Explain Romans 8:28:

   _____

   _____

   _____

   _____

   _____

   _____

Seven Days to Purpose

Seven Days to Purpose

JOURNAL ABOUT IT . . .

Use this section to share the many expressions of gratitude you have for what God has already done in your life. What are you grateful for? Think back to your childhood, create a timeline of gratitude:___

_____
_____
_____
_____
_____
_____
_____
_____
_____
_____
_____
_____
_____

Seven Days to Purpose

Chapter Six: Man

1. Why is it so important to be careful of who and what you are connecting to?

_____

_____

_____

2. What type of people are you drawing into your inner circle?

_____

_____

_____

3. Ephesians 2:10: Who does the text say you are and what were you created to do?

_____

_____

_____

_____

_____

Seven Days to Purpose

JOURNAL ABOUT IT . . .

You are created in the image of God. Explore what that means. What do you need to do to align yourself with how God sees you? _____

_____

_____

_____

_____

_____

_____

_____

_____

_____

_____

_____

_____

_____

Seven Days to Purpose

Chapter Seven: Perfection

1. Read Genesis 2:1-2: What did God do on the seventh day?

   _____

   _____

   _____

2. What has been your prior understanding of perfection?

   _____

   _____

   _____

3. What have you learned about perfection? (Ponder why God rested)

   _____

   _____

   _____

   _____

   _____

Seven Days to Purpose

Seven Days to Purpose

JOURNAL ABOUT IT . . .

It's time to put it all to practice. Create your very own I am declarations here. You can use this later to recite from as you decree who God says you are:

_____
_____
_____
_____
_____
_____
_____
_____
_____
_____
_____
_____
_____
_____
_____

Seven Days to Purpose

QUICK POINTS

Seven Days to Purpose

Seven Days to Purpose

Quick Points to Ponder (for reinforcement) . . .

1. Read John 4:28-30 and John 4:39-42? Explain what has happened here with the Samaritan woman.

Seven Days to Purpose

2. Have you ever experienced such an encounter with the Lord? Share/Explain.

Seven Days to Purpose

3. What is that one thing you would immediately change in your life if you were given the power to do so? Tell how you would do so.

_____
_____
_____
_____
_____
_____
_____
_____
_____
_____
_____
_____
_____
_____
_____
_____

Seven Days to Purpose

NOTES

Johnston, Robert D. <u>Numbers in the Bible</u>: God's Unique Design in Biblical Numbers. Kregel Publications, 1990.

Booking Information

For general information and speaking engagements,

contact Women In Need of Empowerment (W.I.N.E.)

at www.stayonthevine.com or email us here:

info@stayonthevine.com.

> **Women In Need of Empowerment**
> P.O. Box 7303, Hampton VA 23666

www.ingramcontent.com/pod-product-compliance
Lightning Source LLC
Chambersburg PA
CBHW061333040426
42444CB00011B/2901